AF539151

Calm

Down

Published 2026

FiNGERPRINT!

Prakash Books

Fingerprint Publishing
@FingerprintP
@fingerprintpublishingbooks

ISBN: 978 93 5856 476 1

To..................
From..................

Calm . . .

What is calm anyway?

Calmness is simply a mental state of peace
and serenity, wherein you are not affected
by strong emotions.

But why do we need to find peace anyway?

Moreover, in this fast-paced world,
can we even afford to slow down and breathe?

Calmness is often confused with a passive
state of being, but, on the contrary,
it is the greatest strength in disguise.

Achieving peace is not as hard as we think,
and a little encouragement never hurt anyone!

So, Keep Calm and Carry On!

"WHEN SPECULATION HAS DONE ITS WORST, TWO AND TWO STILL MAKE FOUR."

Samuel Johnson

“DEVELOPING CONCERN FOR OTHERS, THINKING OF THEM AS PART OF US, BRINGS SELF-CONFIDENCE, REDUCES OUR SENSE OF SUSPICION AND MISTRUST, AND ENABLES US TO DEVELOP A CALM MIND.”

14th Dalai Lama

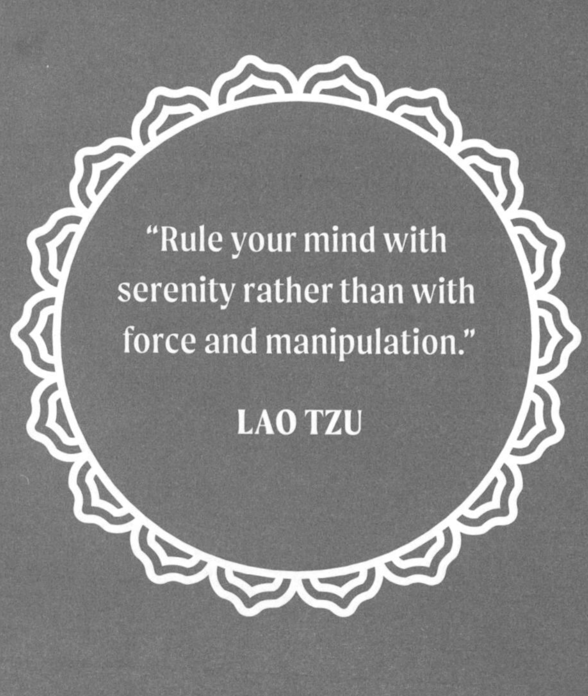
"Rule your mind with serenity rather than with force and manipulation."
LAO TZU

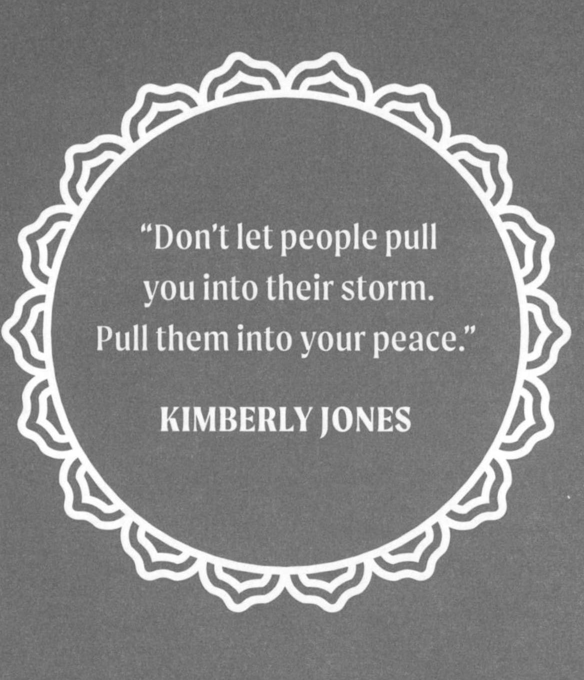
"Don't let people pull
you into their storm.
Pull them into your peace."
KIMBERLY JONES

"If our thoughts are peaceful,
calm, meek, and kind,
then that is what our life is like."

ELDER TADEJ ŠTRBULOVIĆ

"THE NEARER A MAN COMES TO A CALM MIND, THE CLOSER HE IS TO STRENGTH."

Marcus Aurelius

"In calmness lies true pleasure."

Victor Hugo

"Nobody can bring you peace but yourself."

Ralph Waldo Emerson

"I WILL BE CALM.
I WILL BE MISTRESS OF MYSELF."

Jane Austen

"THOSE WHO ACT WITH FEW DESIRES ARE CALM, WITHOUT WORRY OR FEAR."

Buddha

"IN THE TURBULENCE OF LIFE, FIND SOLACE IN THE CALM CENTER WITHIN. BREATHE IN SERENITY, EXHALE CHAOS, AND LET THE STILLNESS BE YOUR SANCTUARY."

Thich Nhat Hanh

“Stay centered by accepting
whatever you are doing.
This is the ultimate.”

CHUANG TZU

"CALMNESS IS NOT THE ABSENCE OF STORMS BUT THE ART OF FINDING PEACE WITHIN THEM."

Jon Kabat-Zinn

"In times of great stress or adversity, it's always best to keep busy, to plow your anger and your energy into something positive."

LEE LACOCCA

"Peace is a daily, a weekly,
a monthly process,
gradually changing opinions,
slowly eroding old barriers,
quietly building new structures."

JOHN F. KENNEDY

"If you are depressed,
you are living in the
past, if you are anxious,
you are living in the future,
if you are at peace, you are
living in the present."

LAO TZU

"When the mind is calm,
how quickly, how smoothly,
how beautifully you will
perceive everything."

**PARAMAHANSA
YOGANANDA**

"Calmness is a skill, a quiet superpower cultivated in the garden of patience. In moments of turmoil, tend to your inner peace and watch the storms subside."

SHARON SALZBERG

"ALL OF HUMANITY'S PROBLEMS STEM FROM MAN'S INABILITY TO SIT QUIETLY IN A ROOM ALONE."

Blaise Pascal

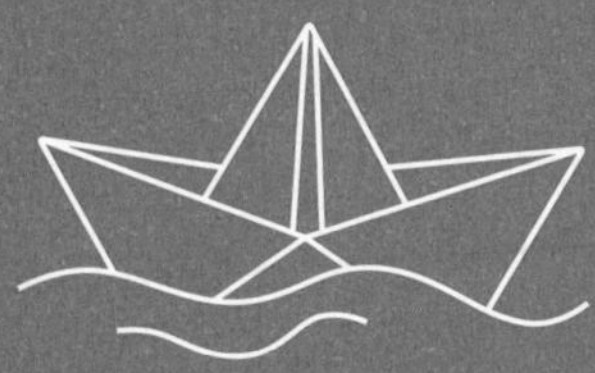

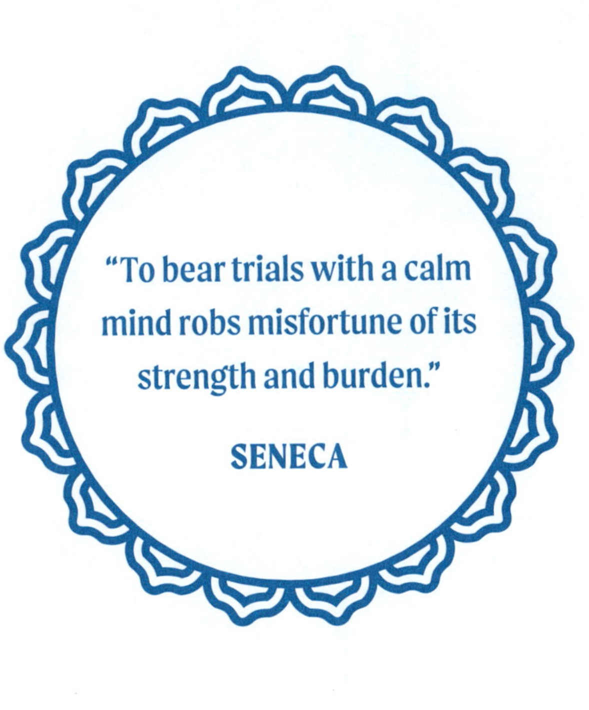
"To bear trials with a calm mind robs misfortune of its strength and burden."
SENECA

“AMIDST THE CHAOS, BECOME THE CALM CONDUCTOR ORCHESTRATING THE SYMPHONY OF YOUR EMOTIONS. ”

Haemin Sunim

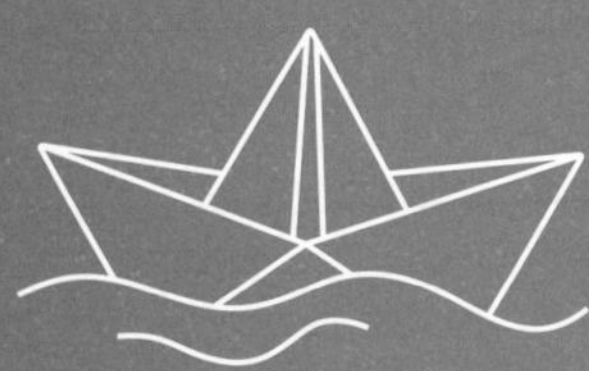

"MY FAVOURITE PIECE OF MUSIC IS THE ONE WE HEAR ALL THE TIME IF WE ARE QUIET."

John Cage

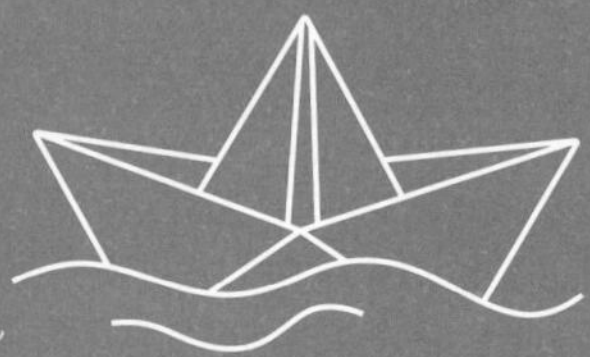

"WHEN THE POWER OF LOVE OVERCOMES THE LOVE OF POWER THE WORLD WILL KNOW PEACE."

Jimi Hendrix

"To be calm is the highest achievement of the self."

ZEN PROVERB

"Do you pay regular visits
to yourself?
Start now."

RUMI

"DECIDE THAT
WHEREVER YOU ARE,
IS THE BEST PLACE THERE IS.
ONCE YOU START COMPARING,
THERE'S NO END TO IT."

Sodo Yokoyama

“TENSION IS
WHO YOU THINK
YOU SHOULD BE.
RELAXATION IS
WHO YOU ARE.”

Chinese Proverb

"Avoid all haste;
calmness is an essential
ingredient of politeness."

Alphonse Karr

"TO THINK TOO MUCH IS A DISEASE."

Fyodor Dostoyevsky

"There will be calmness when one is free from external objects and is not perturbed."

BRUCE LEE

“THE TRUE STRENGTH OF A MAN IS IN CALMNESS.”

Leo Tolstoy

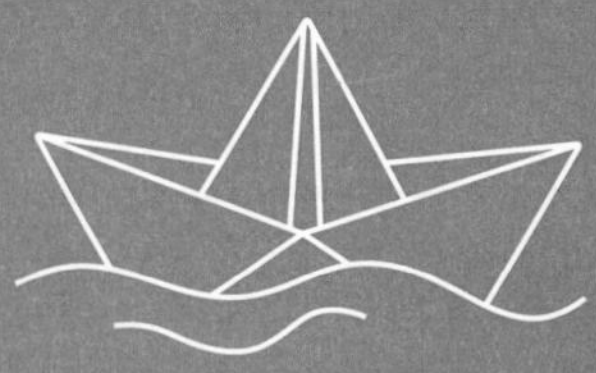

**“SITTING SILENTLY,
DOING NOTHING,
SPRING COMES,
AND THE GRASS
GROWS BY ITSELF.”**

Bashō

"FEARLESSNESS PRESUPPOSES CALMNESS AND PEACE OF MIND."

Mahatma Gandhi

"MY HOPES ARE NOT ALWAYS REALIZED, BUT I ALWAYS HOPE."

Ovid

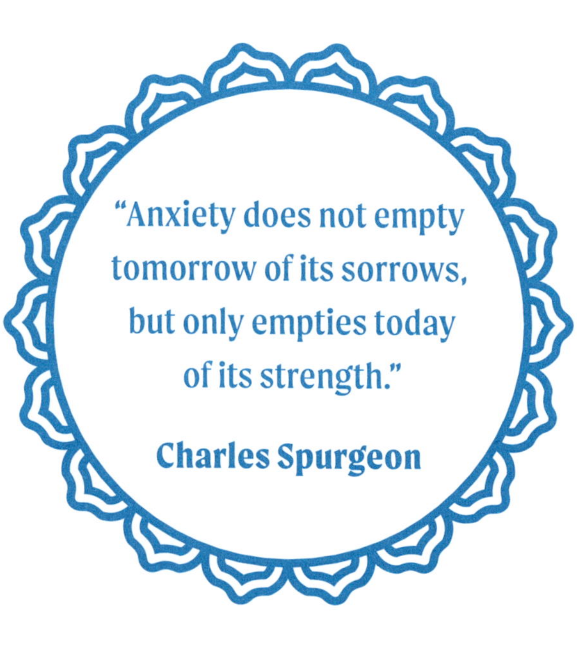
"Anxiety does not empty
tomorrow of its sorrows,
but only empties today
of its strength."
Charles Spurgeon

"FAME AND TRANQUILITY CAN NEVER BE BEDFELLOWS."

Michel de Montaigne

"By three methods
we may learn wisdom:
First, by reflection,
which is noblest;
Second, by imitation,
which is easiest;
and third by experience,
which is the bitterest."

CONFUCIUS

**"THE LIFE OF INNER PEACE,
BEING HARMONIOUS
AND WITHOUT STRESS,
IS THE EASIEST TYPE
OF EXISTENCE."**

Norman Vincent Peale

"Retain a calm heart,
sit like a turtle,
walk swiftly like a pigeon,
and sleep like a dog."

LI CHING-YUEN

“LIFE GOES BY FAST.
ENJOY IT.
CALM DOWN.
IT'S ALL FUNNY.”

Joan Rivers

Why Do You Need to Remain Calm?

- ★ Being calm helps your body to create endorphins, which are hormones that elevate your mood and make you happy!

- ★ Being calm enables you to be in control of the situation. On the other hand, when you panic, you might make rash decisions, which might not benefit you in the long run.

- ★ Being calm helps you become a better communicator. People around you trust you if you are calm in a tough situation.

- ★ When you are in control of your inner self, facing external adversities becomes all the more easy.

"PEACE IS LIBERTY IN TRANQUILITY."

Marcus Tullius Cicero

"SOMETIMES I SITS AND THINKS, AND SOMETIMES I JUST SITS."

A.A. Milne

"We are shaped by our thoughts;
we become what we think.
When the mind is pure,
joy follows like a shadow
that never leaves."

BUDDHA

"WORRYING IS LIKE A ROCKING CHAIR, IT GIVES YOU SOMETHING TO DO, BUT IT GETS YOU NOWHERE."

Glenn Turner

"You are the sky.
Everything else it's
just the weather."

Pema Chödrön

"Stop trying to define
who you are
and just be."

Anonymous

"Ships don't sink because
of the water around them;
ships sink because of the
water that gets in them.
Don't let what's happening
around you get inside you
and weigh you down."

ANONYMOUS

“PEACE CAN BECOME A LENS THROUGH WHICH YOU SEE THE WORLD. BE IT. LIVE IT. RADIATE IT OUT. PEACE IS AN INSIDE JOB.”

Wayne Dyer

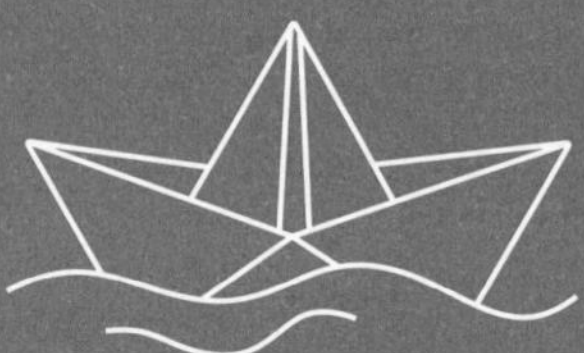

"Worry is a funky luxury
when a lot has to be done."

MELVIN PEEBLES

“CALM IS NOT A DISTANT SHORE; IT’S THE ANCHOR WITHIN. WHEN THE WAVES OF LIFE RISE, DROP YOUR ANCHOR AND LET THE STORM PASS, FOR CALM SEAS AWAIT ON THE OTHER SIDE.”

Matt Haig

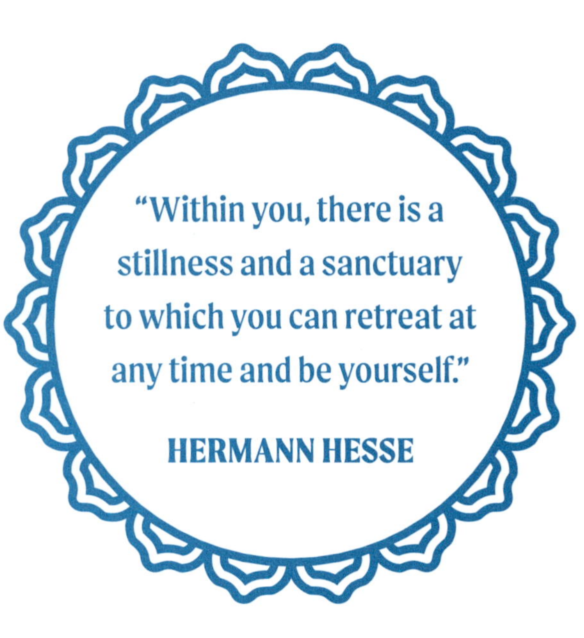
"Within you, there is a
stillness and a sanctuary
to which you can retreat at
any time and be yourself."
HERMANN HESSE

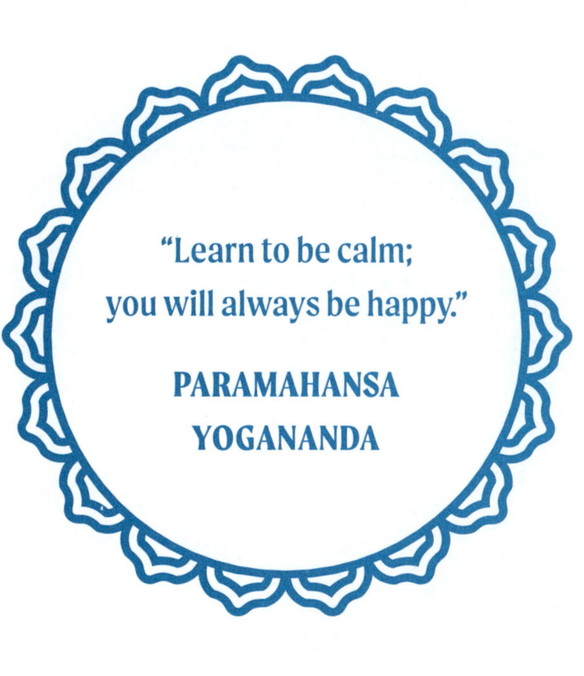
"Learn to be calm;
you will always be happy."
PARAMAHANSA
YOGANANDA

"IT IS DIFFICULT TO MAKE A MAN MISERABLE WHILE HE FEELS WORTHY OF HIMSELF."

Abraham Lincoln

"WHEN THINGS CHANGE
INSIDE YOU,
THINGS CHANGE
AROUND YOU."

Anonymous

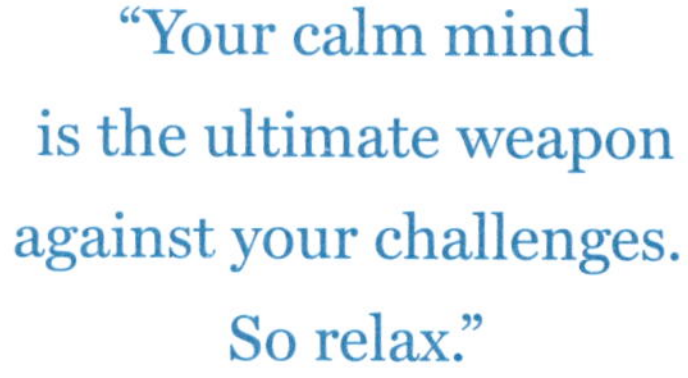

"Your calm mind
is the ultimate weapon
against your challenges.
So relax."

BRYANT MCGILL

"Adopt the pace of nature, her secret is patience."

RALPH WALDO EMERSON

"LET YOUR SOUL STAND COOL AND COMPOSED BEFORE A MILLION UNIVERSES."

Walt Whitman

“THE ORDINARY ACTS
WE PRACTISE EVERYDAY
AT HOME ARE OF MORE
IMPORTANCE TO THE SOUL
THAN THEIR SIMPLICITY
MIGHT SUGGEST.”

Thomas Moore

“HE THAT CAN HAVE PATIENCE CAN HAVE WHAT HE WILL.”

Benjamin Franklin

“BE HAPPY FOR THIS MOMENT. THIS MOMENT IS YOUR LIFE.”

Omar Khayyam

“WE MUST LET GO OF THE LIFE WE HAVE PLANNED, SO AS TO ACCEPT THE ONE THAT IS WAITING FOR US.”

Joseph Campbell

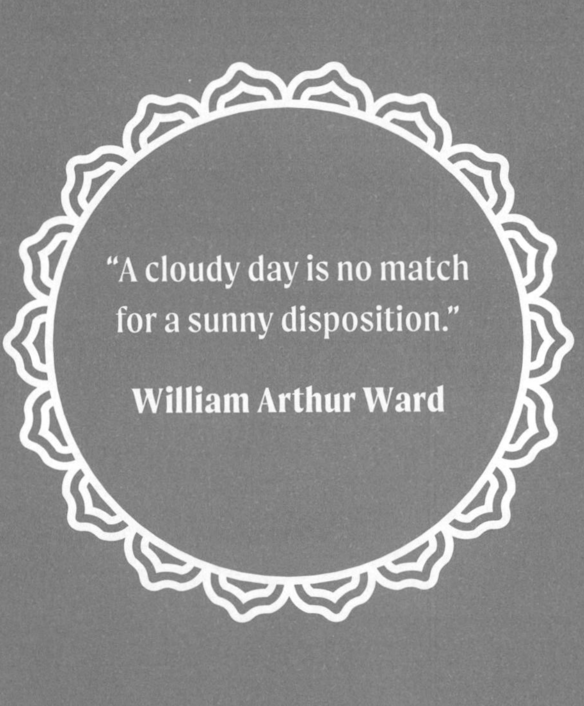
"A cloudy day is no match
for a sunny disposition."
William Arthur Ward

"DO NOT ANTICIPATE TROUBLE, OR WORRY ABOUT WHAT MAY NEVER HAPPEN. KEEP IN THE SUNLIGHT."

Anonymous

“LIFE ISN’T ABOUT FINDING YOURSELF; IT’S ABOUT CREATING YOURSELF.”

George Bernard Shaw

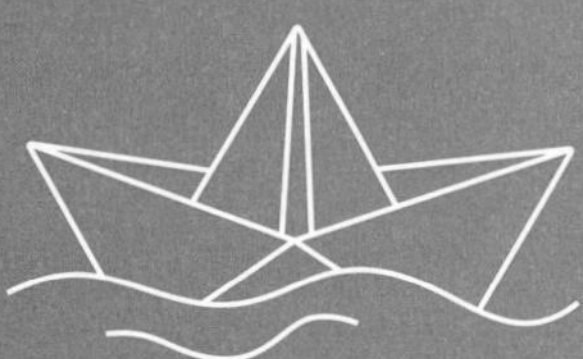

**"NOBODY CAN
MAKE YOU FEEL INFERIOR
WITHOUT YOUR CONSENT."**

Eleanor Roosevelt

**“KIND WORDS
AND GOOD THOUGHTS
WILL UNLOCK IRON DOORS.”**

Turkish Proverb

"Don't try to force anything.
Let life be a deep let-go.
God opens millions
of flowers every day
without forcing their buds."

OSHO

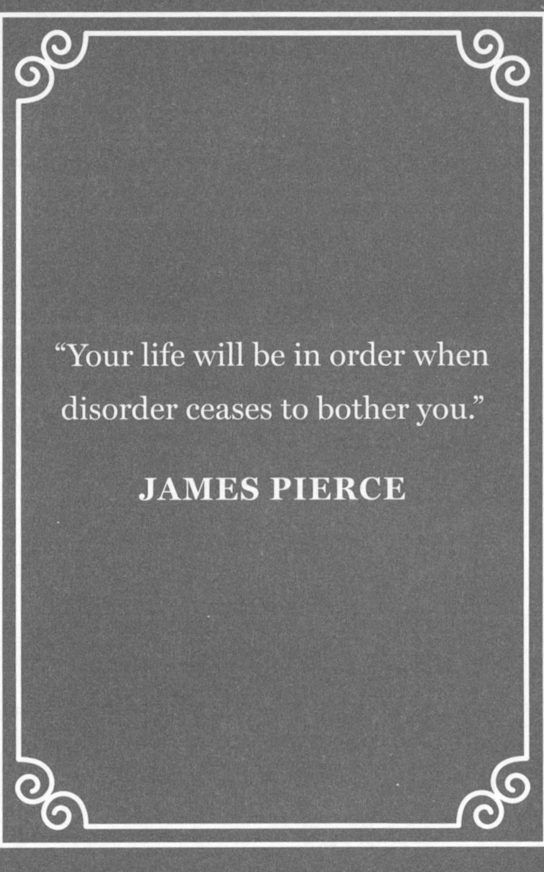

“Your life will be in order when disorder ceases to bother you.”

JAMES PIERCE

"When we are unable
to find tranquility within
ourselves, it is useless
to seek it elsewhere."

FRANÇOIS DE LA ROCHEFOUCAULD

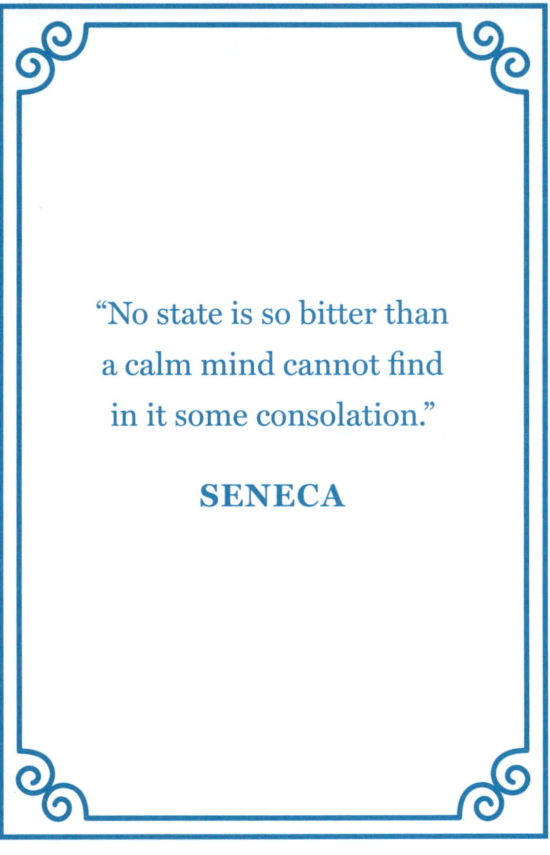

"No state is so bitter than a calm mind cannot find in it some consolation."

SENECA

"Calm mind brings inner strength and self-confidence, so that's very important for good health."

14TH DALAI LAMA

"Nothing diminishes anxiety faster than action."

Walter Anderson

"A SMILE IS THE BEGINNING OF PEACE."

Mother Teresa

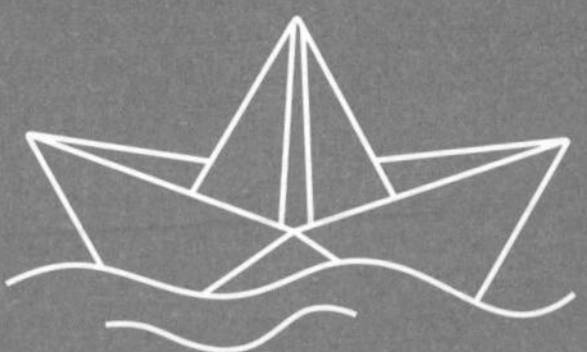

"DO NOT LEARN HOW TO REACT. LEARN HOW TO RESPOND."

Buddha

"You don't have to control your thoughts; you just have to stop letting them control you."

Dan Millman

“SILENCE IS THE ELEMENT IN WHICH GREAT THINGS FASHION THEMSELVES TOGETHER.”

Thomas Carlyle

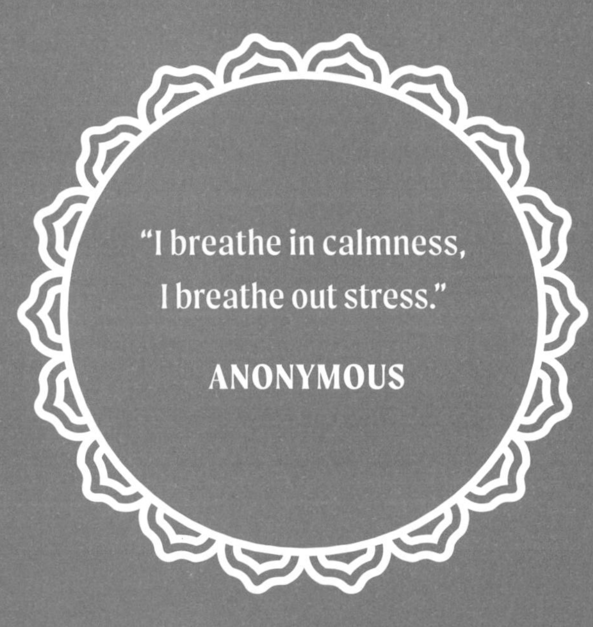
"I breathe in calmness,
I breathe out stress."
ANONYMOUS

"The more tranquil a man becomes, the greater is his success, his influence, his power for good. Calmness of mind is one of the beautiful jewels of wisdom."

JAMES ALLEN

"CALM YOUR MIND;
LIFE BECOMES
MORE CRYSTAL CLEAR."

Anonymous

"Patience is not the ability to wait. Patience is to be calm no matter what happens, constantly take action to turn it to positive growth opportunities, and have faith to believe that it will all work out in the end while you are waiting."

ROY T. BENNETT

“PEACE CANNOT BE KEPT BY FORCE; IT CAN ONLY BE ACHIEVED BY UNDERSTANDING.”

Albert Einstein

"A crust eaten in peace
is better than a banquet
partaken in anxiety."

AESOP

"GET OUT OF YOUR HEAD AND GET INTO YOUR HEART. THINK LESS, FEEL MORE."

Osho

"THOSE WHO ARE POSSESSED BY NOTHING POSSESS EVERYTHING."

Morihei Ueshiba

"Calmness is the ultimate sophistication."

Leonardo da Vinci

"IF THE BLOOD HUMOR IS TOO STRONG AND ROBUST, CALM IT WITH BALANCE AND HARMONY."

Xun Kuang

“CALMNESS IS THE CRADLE OF POWER.”

Josiah Gilbert Holland

“EACH ONE HAS TO FIND HIS PEACE FROM WITHIN. AND PEACE TO BE REAL MUST BE UNAFFECTED BY OUTSIDE CIRCUMSTANCES.”

Mahatma Gandhi

"PEACE IS NOT ABSENCE OF CONFLICT, IT IS THE ABILITY TO HANDLE CONFLICT BY PEACEFUL MEANS."

Ronald Reagan

"CALM SELF-CONFIDENCE IS AS FAR FROM CONCEIT AS THE DESIRE TO EARN A DECENT LIVING IS REMOTE FROM GREED."

Channing Pollock

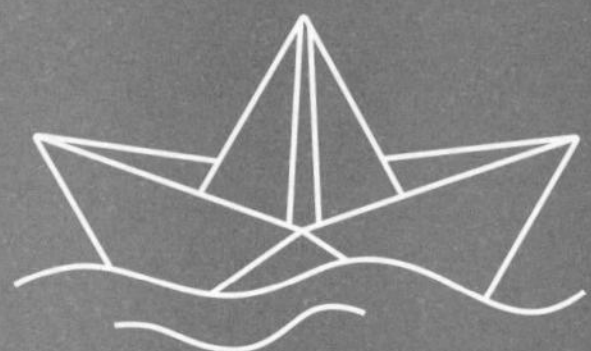

"Nothing gives one person
so much advantage over another
as to remain always cool and
unruffled under all circumstances."

THOMAS JEFFERSON

“When you walk in peace
you will literally see attackers
shattering themselves
against your inner-calm.”

BRYANT MCGILL

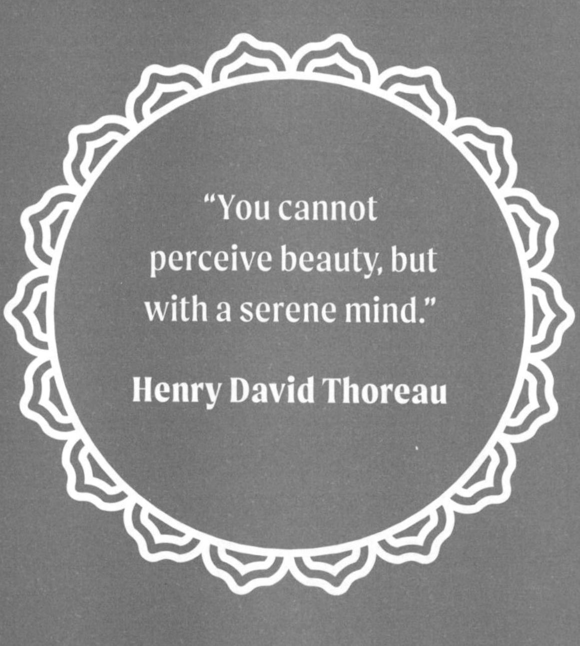
"You cannot perceive beauty, but with a serene mind."
Henry David Thoreau

"THERE CAN BE NO PEACE WITHOUT BUT THROUGH PEACE WITHIN."

W.E. Channing

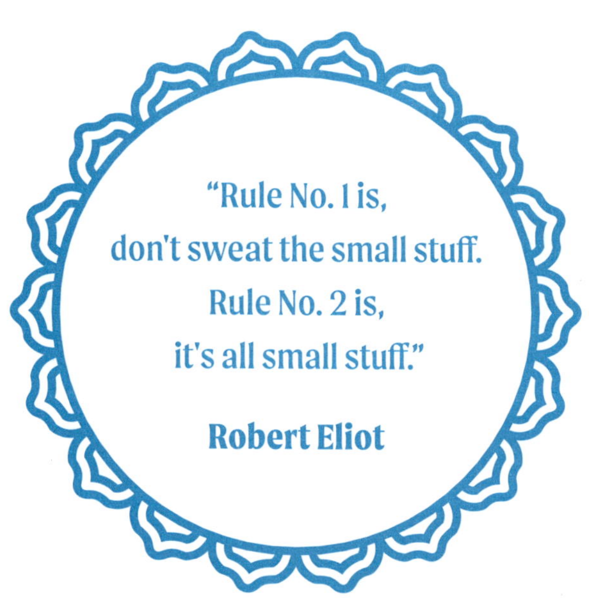
"Rule No. 1 is,
don't sweat the small stuff.
Rule No. 2 is,
it's all small stuff."
Robert Eliot

"Worry affects the circulation, the heart, the glands, the whole nervous system, and profoundly affects the health. You have never known a man who died from overwork, but many who died from doubt."

CHARLES W. MAYO

"Worry is a god,
invisible but omnipotent.
It steals the bloom
from the cheek and
lightness from the pulse;
it takes away the appetite,
and turns the hair gray."

BENJAMIN DISRAELI

“IF YOUR EYES ARE BLINDED WITH YOUR WORRIES, YOU CANNOT SEE THE BEAUTY OF THE SUNSET.”

Jiddu Krishnamurti

“WORRY OFTEN GIVES
A SMALL THING
A BIG SHADOW.”

Swedish Proverb

"If you worry about what
might be, and wonder
what might have been,
you will ignore what is."

ANONYMOUS

"The universe is
not outside of you.
Look inside yourself,
everything that you want,
you already are."

RUMI

"Worries are the most
stubborn habits in the world.
Even after a poor man
has won a huge lottery prize,
he will still for months wake
up in the night with a start,
worrying about food and rent."

VICKI BAUM

"A hundred load of worry
will not pay an ounce of debt."

George Herbert

"It ain't no use putting up your umbrella till it rains!"

Alice Caldwell Rice

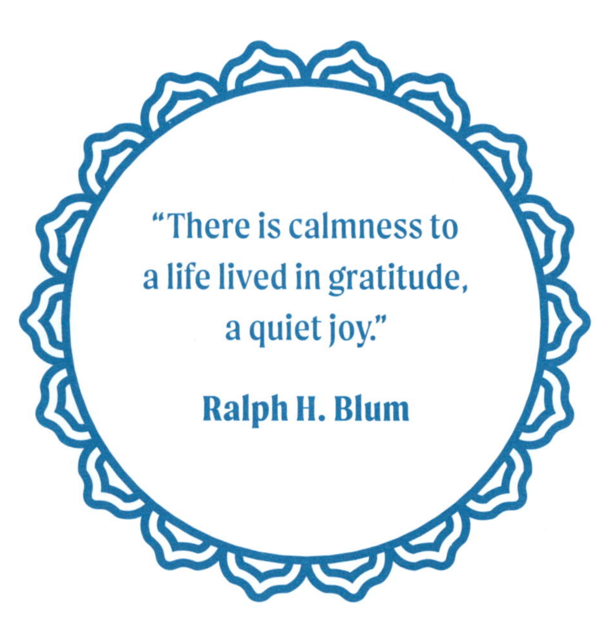

"There is calmness to a life lived in gratitude, a quiet joy."

Ralph H. Blum

"WORRY IS EVIDENCE OF AN ILL-CONTROLLED BRAIN; IT IS MERELY A STUPID WASTE OF TIME IN UNPLEASANTNESS."

Arnold Bennett

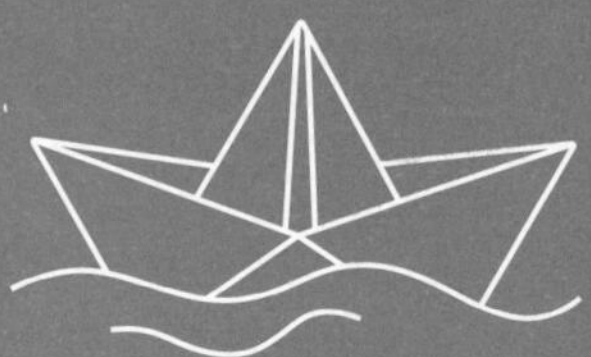

"The quieter you become,
the more you can hear."

RAM DASS

"Peace is the result of
retraining your mind to
process life as it is, rather
than as you think it should be."

WAYNE DYER

Accept that perfectionism is a myth

Get at least eight hours of sleep at night

Maintain a journal

Practice gratitude

Breathe

Read a book

Meditate

Train your brain to be calm in any situation

Spend time with loved one

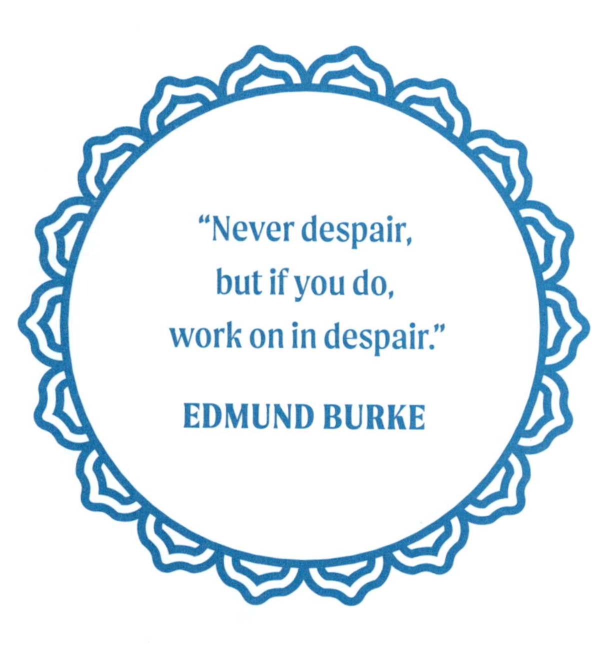
"Never despair,
but if you do,
work on in despair."
EDMUND BURKE

"The ideal of calm exists in a sitting cat."

Jules Renard

"INSIDE MYSELF IS A PLACE WHERE I LIVE ALL ALONE, AND THAT'S WHERE YOU RENEW MY SPRINGS THAT NEVER DRY UP."

Pearl S. Buck

"THE GREATEST WEAPON AGAINST STRESS IS OUR ABILITY TO CHOOSE ONE THOUGHT OVER ANOTHER."

William James

“The mind is like water.

When it’s turbulent,

it’s difficult to see.

When it’s calm,

everything becomes clear.”

PRASAD MAHES

“HOW BEAUTIFUL IT IS
TO DO NOTHING, AND THEN
TO REST AFTERWARDS.”

Spanish Proverb

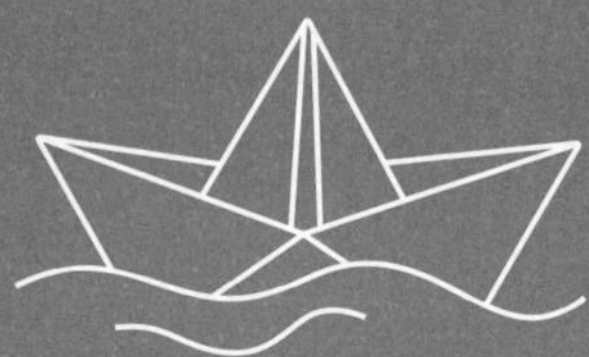

"More smiling, less worrying.
More compassion, less judgment.
More blessed, less stressed.
More love, less hate."

ROY T. BENNETT

"You may not control all the events that happen to you, but you can decide not to be reduced by them."

MAYA ANGELOU

"Life is really simple,
but we insist on
making it complicated."

Confucius

**“YOUR MIND WILL
ANSWER MOST QUESTIONS
IF YOU LEARN TO RELAX
AND WAIT FOR THE ANSWERS.”**

William S. Burroughs

"TODAY START YOUR
DAY WITH A SMILE,
CALMNESS OF MIND,
COOLNESS OF EMOTIONS,
AND A HEART FILLED
WITH GRATITUDE."

Anonymous

“THE ABILITY TO BE IN THE PRESENT MOMENT IS A MAJOR COMPONENT OF MENTAL WELLNESS.”

Abraham Maslow

"PEACE IS NOT A DESTINATION; IT'S A STATE OF MIND. IN THE MIDST OF LIFE'S TURBULENCE, FIND YOUR CENTER, AND LET THE RIPPLES OF CALMNESS SPREAD AROUND YOU."

Marianne Williamson

"Is it so small a thing
to have enjoyed the sun,
to have lived light in the spring
to have loved,
to have thought,
to have done?"

MATTHEW ARNOLD

"Simplify. Stop bothering with the non-essentials."

Anonymous

“MY HEART IS TUNED TO THE QUIETNESS THAT THE STILLNESS OF NATURE INSPIRES.”

Hazrat Inayat Khan

"Calmness is a huge gift.
And once you master it,
you will be able to
respond in a useful way to
every difficult situation
that decides to walk
into your heart."

GERI LARKIN

**"BREATH IS THE POWER
BEHIND ALL THINGS.
I BREATHE IN AND KNOW THAT
GOOD THINGS WILL HAPPEN."**

Tao Porchon-Lynch

"ONE WHO IS AT PEACE
CAN DRAW GOOD
FROM EVERYTHING."

Gerhard Groote

"THERE ARE SOME THINGS YOU LEARN BEST IN CALM, AND SOME IN STORM."

Willa Cather

"I want to tell people that they should always try to stay calm and speak good things, have control over food by adopting healthy food habits, eat less food and exercise daily."

MILKHA SINGH

"Sometimes you can find peace of mind by transferring yourself to different situations. They're just reminders to stay calm."

YVES BEHAR

"There will be calmness,
tranquility when one is free
from external objects
and is not perturbed."

BRUCE LEE

"WHEN THE ODDS ARE HOPELESS, WHEN ALL SEEMS TO BE LOST, THEN IS THE TIME TO BE CALM."

Ian Fleming

"Calm can solve all issues."

POPE SHENOUDA III

"The secret of success is to be in harmony with existence, to be always calm to let each wave of life wash us a little farther up the shore."

CYRIL CONNOLLY

"LOOKING FOR PEACE
IS LIKE LOOKING FOR A
TURTLE WITH A MUSTACHE:
YOU WON'T BE ABLE TO FIND IT.
BUT WHEN YOUR HEART
IS READY, PEACE WILL COME
LOOKING FOR YOU."

Ajahn Chah

"CALMNESS IS THE ELIXIR OF THE SOUL, DISTILLED THROUGH PATIENCE AND SIPPED IN MOMENTS OF QUIET REFLECTION."

Pico Iyer

"CALMNESS IS THE RAREST QUALITY IN HUMAN LIFE. IT IS THE POISE OF A GREAT NATURE, IN HARMONY WITH ITSELF AND ITS IDEALS."

Annie Besant

"To be interested in
the changing seasons is
a happier state of mind
than to be hopelessly
in love with spring."

GEORGE SANTAYANA

"HE IS THE HAPPIEST,
BE HE KING, OR PEASANT,
WHO FINDS PEACE IN HIS HOME."

Johann Wolfgang
Von Gothe

"IF HE CANNOT STOP THE MIND THAT SEEKS AFTER FAME AND PROFIT, HE WILL SPEND HIS LIFE WITHOUT FINDING PEACE."

Dogen

"The most intense conflicts,
if overcome, leave behind
a sense of security and calm
that is not easily disturbed.
It is just these intense conflicts
and their conflagration which
are needed to produce
valuable and lasting results."

CARL JUNG

“CALMNESS IS THE BEAUTY OF LIFE. IT IS THE SOURCE OF ENTHUSIASM, STRENGTH, AND INSPIRATION.”

PARAMAHANSA YOGANANDA

"BE LIKE A DUCK.
CALM ON THE SURFACE,
BUT ALWAYS PADDLING LIKE
THE DICKENS UNDERNEATH."

MICHAEL CAINE

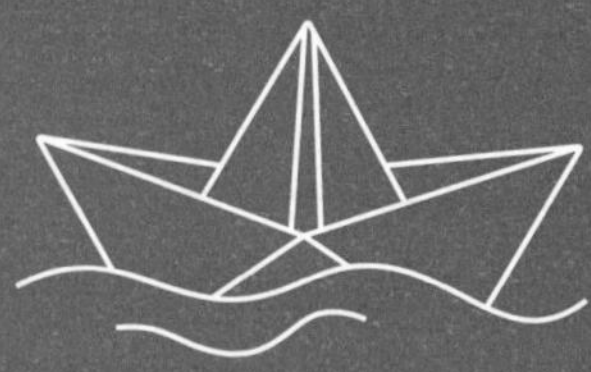

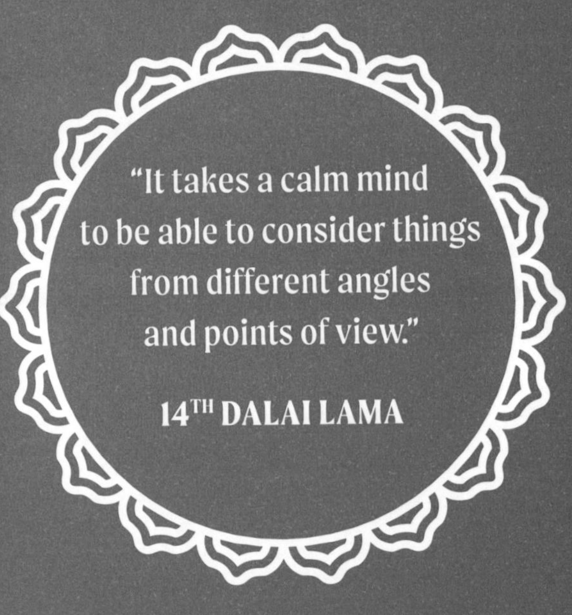
"It takes a calm mind
to be able to consider things
from different angles
and points of view."
14TH DALAI LAMA

"A fit body, a calm mind, a house full of love. These things cannot be bought. They must be earned."

NAVAL RAVIKANTH

"UNDERSTAND: PRESENCE OF MIND IS THE ABILITY TO DETACH YOURSELF, TO SEE THE WHOLE BATTLEFIELD, THE WHOLE PICTURE, WITH CLARITY."

Robert Greene

"WORRY NEVER ROBS TOMORROW OF ITS SORROW, IT ONLY SAPS TODAY OF ITS JOY."

Leo F. Buscaglia